Reading Plus 3

Clue & Key

CONTENTS

# Scope and Sequence

	Title	Topic		Text Type
1	Treasure Island		Sailing	Classic tales
2	Creatures of the Deep	Ocean	Ocean animals	Nonfiction
3	Shark Attack!		Sharks	Fiction
4	Coral Reefs		Coral	Nonfiction
5	The Shoemaker and the Elves		Shoemaker	Classic tales
6	Leonardo da Vinci	Job	Renaissance man	Nonfiction
7	Rachel's Busy Day		Chefs	Fiction
8	Jobs of the Future		Future jobs	Nonfiction
9	The Miser and His Gold		Miser	Aesop's fables
10	Who Donated the Money?	Money	Donor	Nonfiction
11	The World's Richest Man		Money sharing	Fiction
12	The History of Money		History of money	Nonfiction
13	The Little Prince		The planets	Classic tales
14	Aliens in Stories and Movies	Space	Aliens	Nonfiction
15	A Visit to Mars		Space travel	Fiction
16	Apollo 11		The moon	Nonfiction

Grammar	Vocabulary
when	crew, discover, hire, inn, pirate, possession
used to	attract, creature, fascinating, fin, pressure, stretch
past continuous	bottom, crab, disappear, escape, jaw, shadow
will be able to	area, lay, nutrient, predator, provide, shallow
plurals	continue, curious, dawn, elf, stitch, workshop
too / either	cannon, complete, invent, sculpture, take place, weapon
prepositions of time	assist, complain, satisfied, shrimp, supply, throw away
there will be	advanced, industry, society, space, technology, tourism
possessive pronouns	alone, bury, coin, lock, miser, overhear
question words	anonymous, donation, financial, homeless, lose, receive
make	electronics, employee, own, salary, share, wealthy
how to + verb	carry, check, firewood, melt, metal, trade
and	bite, desert, encounter, lie, odd, planet
no one	alien, destroy, fiction, mean, monstrous, murder
adjective order	astronaut, communicate, land, Mars, peace, translate
prepositions of movement	act, amazing, hero, launch, reach, satellite

Treasure Island

Before You Read

Read and check.

	True	False
1. Gold and silver are treasures.	☐	☐
2. An island is a building.	☐	☐
3. A crew works on a ship.	☐	☐

New Words 02

Listen and repeat.

1 pirate:

2 inn: a small hotel

3 crew: the workers on a ship

4 hire: to give a job to someone

5 discover: to find out

6 possession: something a person owns

New Sentences

Write a, b, or c.

1 ☐ Jim discovers they are pirates.

2 ☐ Jim Hawkins is working at his family's inn.

3 ☐ Jim goes through the man's possessions.

Treasure Island

Jim Hawkins is working at his family's inn when a mysterious man arrives. But that man soon dies. So Jim goes through the man's possessions and finds a treasure map. Jim and his friends purchase a ship, the *Hispaniola*. Then they hire some crews. The ship's cook is Long John Silver, a man with one leg.

They sail to the island. While on the ship, Jim hears Silver talking with some other crew members. He discovers they are pirates. They plan to find the treasure, steal it, and kill Jim and his friends. When they get to the island, Jim and the others run away from the pirates. They have several battles with the pirates. In the end, the pirates lose. Jim and the others find the treasure. They leave Silver and the pirates on the island and sail back home as rich men.

Listening Quiz! 04

1 ⓐ Yes   ⓑ No

2 ⓐ a pirate   ⓑ Jim's friend

Details

Choose or write the answer.

1 Jim goes through the man's possessions and finds a _____ map.

    ⓐ pirate   ⓑ treasure   ⓒ gold   ⓓ crew

2 They sail to the _____ to find the treasure.

    ⓐ island   ⓑ inn   ⓒ map   ⓓ ship

3 Who only has one leg?

    ⓐ Jim Hawkins   ⓑ the mysterious man   ⓒ Long John Silver   ⓓ Hispaniola

4 What do Jim and his friends find on the island?

    - They find the _____.

Main Idea

Choose the main idea.

    ⓐ Long John Silver has only one leg.

    ⓑ Some pirates attack Jim Hawkins and his friends.

    ⓒ Jim and others defeat some pirates and find the treasure.

    ⓓ Long John Silver has to stay on the island without any treasure.

Organizing

Put the events in order.

◯   Jim's side wins and leaves the island.

◯   They sail to the island.

◯   On the island, pirates fight Jim and the others.

◯   Jim and his friends buy a ship.

Vocabulary

Fill in the blanks.

> inn   possession   hire   crew   discover   pirate

1 The picture of my family is my most valuable _____.

2 The ship's _____ had to work hard during the hurricane.

3 We stayed at an _____ for the night when we were traveling.

4 The _____ sailed his ship on the ocean and looked for treasure.

5 The manager said that they wanted to _____ Susan.

6 We have to _____ where the money is.

Summary 05

Listen to the summary and fill in the blanks.

A _____ man visits Jim Hawkins's _____. He dies, and Jim finds a

treasure map in his _____. Jim and his friends _____ to the treasure

island. But the ship's _____ are all pirates. They fight Jim and the others for

the _____. But Jim's side wins and becomes rich.

 Tip **One-Minute Grammar!**

When has the same meaning as "at the time." You can connect two sentences by using **when**.

Jim Hawkins is working at his family's inn **when** a mysterious man arrives.

Creatures of the Deep

Before You Read

Read and check.

	True	False
1. Many animals live in the ocean.	☐	☐
2. The ocean is very deep.	☐	☐
3. Humans live in the ocean.	☐	☐

New Words 🔊 06

Listen and repeat.

❶ **fin:**

❷ **creature:** an animal

❸ **fascinating:** interesting

❹ **attract:** to draw toward

❺ **pressure:** pressing on something

❻ **stretch:** to become longer or wider

New Sentences

Write a, b, or c.

❶ ☐ The lanternfish can make its own light to attract other fish.

❷ ☐ It looks like it has legs instead of fins.

❸ ☐ Many unique creatures live deep beneath the ocean.

Creatures of the Deep

- Topic: Ocean Animals
- Genre: Nonfiction

In some places, the ocean is thousands of meters deep. Deep in the ocean, there's no light, and the water pressure is very high. Scientists used to think nothing lived there. But, in fact, many unique creatures live deep beneath the ocean.

Viper fish live deep in the ocean. Some have huge eyes, and others can make their own light. They usually have long, sharp teeth. The gulper eel is another fascinating deep-sea creature. It has a stomach that can stretch so far that it can eat fish even bigger than it is!

Like the viper fish, the lanternfish can make its own light. It does that to attract other fish to catch and eat them. The coelacanth lives deep under water, too. It even looks like it has legs instead of fins. How unique!

lanternfish

viper fish

gulper eel

coelacanth

Listening Quiz! ● 08

1 ⓐ Yes   ⓑ No

2 ⓐ gulper eel   ⓑ lanternfish

Details

Choose or write the answer.

1 Deep in the ocean, the water _____ is very high.

ⓐ power   ⓑ light   ⓒ pressure   ⓓ temperature

2 The lanternfish can make its own _____.

ⓐ food   ⓑ light   ⓒ fins   ⓓ stomach

3 What fish has fins that look like legs?

ⓐ the viper fish   ⓑ the lanternfish   ⓒ the coelacanth   ⓓ the gulper eel

4 What is special about the gulper eel's stomach?

- It can _____ so far that it can eat fish even bigger than it is.

Main Idea

Choose the main idea.

ⓐ A lot of different kinds of fish live deep in the ocean.

ⓑ The viper fish is the most unusual deep-sea creature.

ⓒ There is no light thousands of meters below the ocean surface.

ⓓ The coelacanth looks like it has legs, not fins.

Organizing

Complete the chart.

Kinds of Fish	Unique Characteristics
_____	huge eyes; long, sharp _____; can make its own light
gulper eel	has a _____ that can stretch very far
_____	looks like it has legs instead of fins

Vocabulary

Fill in the blanks.

> pressure   creature   fascinating   stretch   attract   fins

1. You should always _____ your body before exercising.

2. One of a shark's _____ is the part that sticks out above the water.

3. The snake is an interesting _____ ; it doesn't have any legs.

4. The air _____ falls before it rains.

5. Blood in the water can _____ sharks from far away.

6. The documentary was _____ . We couldn't stop watching it.

Summary 09

Listen to the summary and fill in the blanks.

Deep beneath the _____, the water _____ is high. But there are many

fascinating _____. The viper fish and lanternfish make their own light. The

light _____ other fish for them to _____ and eat. The gulper eel's

stomach can stretch far. And the coelacanth has fins that resemble _____.

🔔 Tip One-Minute Grammar!

Use **used to** to talk about what you did in the past but do not do anymore.

Scientists **used to** think nothing lived there.
Mary **used to** live in London.

Shark Attack!

Read and check.

	True	False
1. Sharks live in lakes.	☐	☐
2. A dolphin is a very small fish.	☐	☐
3. People can scuba dive in the ocean.	☐	☐

New Words ● 10

Listen and repeat.

1 crab:

2 shadow:

3 jaw:

4 escape: to get away from

5 disappear: to go away

6 bottom: the floor of something

New Sentences

Write a, b, or c.

a  **b**  **c**

1 ☐ The shark opened its jaws.

2 ☐ They swam down to the bottom.

3 ☐ There was a big shadow above them.

Shark Attack!

• Topic: Sharks
• Genre: Fiction

"Are you ready to go scuba diving?" asked Rick. "Yeah, the water looks great. Let's jump in," answered Sharon. Rick and Sharon dived into the water. They swam down to the bottom. There were all kinds of fish in the ocean. They saw colorful fish, big and small fish, crabs, lobsters, and other sea creatures.

Suddenly, all the fish disappeared. Rick and Sharon looked around. There was a big shadow above them. It was a shark! They were both scared. The shark was circling around them. It was getting closer and closer. The shark opened its jaws. It had huge teeth! Just then, two other big fish swam toward the shark. They were dolphins! They attacked the shark. They hit it with their noses. Rick and Sharon escaped and swam up to the boat. "I hate sharks, but I love dolphins," said Sharon.

Listening Quiz! 12

1 ⓐ Yes   ⓑ No

2 ⓐ the ocean   ⓑ a river

Choose or write the answer.

1 Rick and Sharon swam down to the _____.

   ⓐ bottom   ⓑ shadows   ⓒ surface   ⓓ boat

2 The shark was _____ around them.

   ⓐ jumping   ⓑ biting   ⓒ circling   ⓓ escaping

3 Who attacked the shark?

   ⓐ Rick   ⓑ Sharon   ⓒ dolphins   ⓓ crabs

4 What did Rick and Sharon see at the bottom?

   - They saw colorful fish, big and small fish, crabs, _____, etc.

Main Idea

Choose the main idea.

   ⓐ Rick and Sharon went scuba diving in the ocean.
   ⓑ Some dolphins and a shark were swimming together.
   ⓒ A shark started circling Rick and Sharon.
   ⓓ Some dolphins saved Rick and Sharon from a shark.

Organizing

Put the events in order.

   ◯ A shark started to circle around Rick and Sharon.

   ◯ Rick and Sharon escaped from the shark.

   ◯ Two dolphins attacked the shark.

   ◯ Rick and Sharon dived to the sea bottom and saw many fish.

Vocabulary

Fill in the blanks.

> crab   bottom   escape   shadow   jaw   disappear

1. The magician made a rabbit _____ in his hat.

2. The prisoner is trying to _____ from the jail.

3. One of my favorite meals is _____ legs.

4. My _____ hurts because I was chewing gum all day long.

5. Your _____ gets longer when the sun is low in the sky.

6. Can you swim down to the _____ of the pool?

Summary 13

Listen to the summary and fill in the blanks.

Rick and Sharon went scuba _____ in the ocean. They dived to the _____

and saw many fish. Suddenly, all the fish _____, and they saw a huge

_____. A shark started circling them. Then, two _____ came and

attacked the shark. So Rick and Sharon _____ from the shark.

🔔 Tip One-Minute Grammar!

Use the past continuous tense to talk about something you were doing in the past.
was/were + verb -ing

The shark **was circling** around them.
They **were swimming** in the water.

Coral Reefs

Before You Read

Read and check.

	True	False
1. Coral reefs are in the pond.	☐	☐
2. Sharks kill and eat small fish.	☐	☐
3. Pollution can make the water dirty.	☐	☐

New Words 🔊 14

Listen and repeat.

1 lay:

2 provide: to offer

3 shallow: low

4 area: a place

5 nutrient: substance that is good for health

6 predator: an animal that kills and eats other animals

New Sentences

Write a, b, or c.

  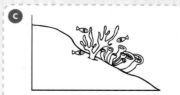

1 ☐ Many fish lay their eggs in coral reefs.

2 ☐ Coral reefs provide safe places for fish to live.

3 ☐ Predators like sharks can't swim in the reefs.

Coral Reefs

Some shallow parts of the ocean have coral reefs. Coral looks like a hard, rocky plant. But it's actually a living creature. When millions of coral come together in one area, they create a coral reef. Coral reefs are very important for the oceans.

First, coral reefs provide safe places for fish to live. Large numbers of species of fish often live in the reefs. Predators like sharks can't swim in the reefs. So the fish are safe there. For that reason, many fish lay their eggs in coral reefs. Coral reefs are also rich in food. They are typically found in warm waters. The water around a reef has many nutrients. This provides food for the fish.

Unfortunately, people and pollution are destroying coral reefs. People need to take better care of the coral reefs. Then, more fish will be able to live in the ocean.

Listening Quiz! 16

1 ⓐ Yes   ⓑ No

2 ⓐ a creature   ⓑ a plant

Details

Choose or write the answer.

1 Coral reefs provide _____ places for fish to live.

    ⓐ shallow   ⓑ dirty   ⓒ dangerous   ⓓ safe

2 The water around a reef has many _____.

    ⓐ nutrients   ⓑ sharks   ⓒ oceans   ⓓ eggs

3 What do fish often do in coral reefs?

    ⓐ sleep   ⓑ lay eggs   ⓒ hunt   ⓓ pollute

4 What is destroying coral reefs these days?

    - People and _____ are destroying coral reefs.

Main Idea

Choose the main idea.

    ⓐ Sharks are unable to swim into coral reefs.

    ⓑ Humans need to take better care of coral reefs.

    ⓒ Coral reefs provide homes and food for fish.

    ⓓ Coral reefs usually only grow in warm, shallow water.

Organizing

Complete the chart.

Coral Reef

- is a living _____
- lives in a _____ part of the ocean
- provides _____ places for fish to live
- provides _____ for fish

Fill in the blanks.

> shallow　area　predator　provide　lay　nutrients

1 Can you _____ some help for us, please?

2 The body needs _____ in order to survive.

3 Turtles _____ their eggs in the sand.

4 What _____ of Korea do you come from?

5 A lion is a dangerous _____ that lives in Africa.

6 The _____ end of the swimming pool is only three feet deep.

Summary 17

Listen to the summary and fill in the blanks.

Coral reefs are in warm, shallow ocean water. Corals look like _____ but are

alive. Coral reefs _____ safe places for millions of animals. Animals can hide

from _____ like sharks there. They can _____ eggs and eat plenty of

food. But humans and _____ are _____ coral reefs nowadays.

Tip One-Minute Grammar!

Use **will be able to** to talk about a future action. It has a similar meaning with **can**. But it refers to the future.

More fish **will be able to** live in the ocean.
You **will be able to** make new friends.

The Shoemaker and the Elves

Read and check.

	True	False
1. A shoemaker makes belts.	☐	☐
2. Some shoes are made of leather.	☐	☐
3. Elves are magical being in children's stories.	☐	☐

New Words 18

Listen and repeat.

1 **elf:**

2 **stitch:**

3 **curious:** eager to know

4 **dawn:** the time when the sun rises

5 **continue:** to keep doing something

6 **workshop:** a place where a person works

New Sentences

Write a, b, or c.

1 ☐ The shoemaker was curious about the new shoes.

2 ☐ Around midnight, three elves visited his workshop.

3 ☐ An old shoemaker cut leather and stitched them together.

The Shoemaker and the Elves

• Topic: Shoemaker
• Genre: Classic Tales

An old shoemaker cut leather and stitched them together to make shoes every day. But he was still very poor. One day, he only had enough leather for one pair of shoes. He cut the leather and went to bed.

In the morning, he found a brand-new pair of very well-made shoes. A customer came in, saw the shoes, and paid a high price for them. The shoemaker purchased enough leather for two pairs of shoes. The next day, he found two new excellent pairs of shoes. This continued for many days. The shoemaker was curious about the new shoes. So, one night, he stayed up late and hid. Around midnight, three elves visited his workshop. They made shoes all night long and left at dawn. The shoemaker never saw the elves again. But everything went well with him from that time.

Listening Quiz! 20

1 ⓐ Yes   ⓑ No

2 ⓐ two   ⓑ three

Details

Choose or write the answer.

1 The shoemaker only had enough _____ for one pair of shoes.

   ⓐ elves   ⓑ money   ⓒ leather   ⓓ customers

2 The shoemaker was _____ about the new shoes.

   ⓐ curious   ⓑ angry   ⓒ scared   ⓓ surprised

3 When did the elves visit the workshop?

   ⓐ noon   ⓑ evening   ⓒ midnight   ⓓ dawn

4 When did the elves leave the workshop?

   - They left at _____.

Main Idea

Choose the main idea.

   ⓐ A shoemaker hired some elves to come and work for him.

   ⓑ Some elves made shoes every night for an old shoemaker.

   ⓒ A shoemaker didn't have much money to buy leather.

   ⓓ There was enough leather to make two pairs of shoes.

Organizing

Complete the chart.

Main Characters	Place	Events
a shoemaker and three _____	the shoemaker's _____	The elves made _____ every night.

Vocabulary

Fill in the blanks.

> curious   stitch   continued   elf   workshop   dawn

1. The children are very ▭▭▭▭▭▭ about their Christmas presents.

2. You must ▭▭▭▭▭▭ the cloth carefully to make new clothes.

3. The engineer goes to his ▭▭▭▭▭▭ and does his job every day.

4. My mother wakes up at ▭▭▭▭▭▭ and then goes jogging.

5. His speech ▭▭▭▭▭▭ for two hours, so I felt bored.

6. An ▭▭▭▭▭▭ is an imaginary creature that appears in fairy tales.

Summary 🔘 21

Listen to the summary and fill in the blanks.

A shoemaker had enough _____ for one pair of shoes. The next day, he found

a new _____ of shoes in his _____. A customer bought them. Every day,

there were more shoes. The curious shoemaker _____ in his workshop. At

midnight, three _____ came and made shoes until dawn, then _____.

Tip One-Minute Grammar!

Add **s** to make the plural forms of many nouns.
But other nouns have different plural forms.

elf	⟶	**elves**
man	⟶	**men**
sheep	⟶	**sheep**

Leonardo da Vinci

Before You Read

Read and check.

	True	False
1. Leonardo da Vinci was a king.	☐	☐
2. Leonardo da Vinci lived during the Renaissance.	☐	☐
3. Mona Lisa was a painter.	☐	☐

New Words ● 22

Listen and repeat.

① **sculpture:**

② **cannon:**

③ **take place:** to happen

④ **invent:** to make for the first time

⑤ **complete:** perfect

⑥ **weapon:** something used to fight with

New Sentences

Write a, b, or c.

 a

 b

 c

① ☐ He invented lots of weapons like cannons and guns.

② ☐ He also made sculptures.

③ ☐ Leonardo da Vinci was a complete Renaissance man.

Leonardo da Vinci

• Topic: Renaissance Ma[n]
• Genre: Nonfiction

In the 14th century, the Renaissance took place. During this time, there were so many new subjects that some people tried to study. People called someone who could do many jobs a "Renaissance man." Leonardo da Vinci was a complete Renaissance man.

Leonardo could do many things. He was a great painter. He painted the *Mona Lisa*, the most famous painting in the world. He also made sculptures and drew. But he wasn't just an artist. He was a writer and scientist too. Leonardo learned a lot about the human body. He had many great ideas. So he was an inventor and designer as well. He invented lots of different weapons, like cannons and guns. He even designed a helicopter and an airplane. He was a really busy man!

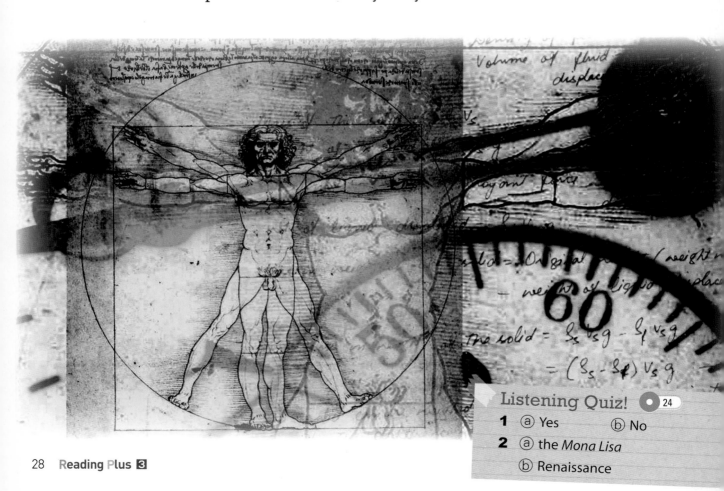

Listening Quiz! 🔊 24

1 ⓐ Yes　　　ⓑ No
2 ⓐ the *Mona Lisa*
　　ⓑ Renaissance

Details

Choose or write the answer.

1 People called someone who could do many jobs a " _____ man."

ⓐ da Vinci   ⓑ Renaissance   ⓒ sculpture   ⓓ busy

2 Leonardo learned a lot about the _____ body.

ⓐ insect   ⓑ animal   ⓒ fish   ⓓ human

3 What is the *Mona Lisa*?

ⓐ a painting   ⓑ a sculpture   ⓒ a sketch   ⓓ a cannon

4 What machines did Leonardo design?

\- He designed a helicopter and an _____.

Main Idea

Choose the main idea.

ⓐ Leonardo da Vinci lived during the Renaissance.

ⓑ A Renaissance man is not good at many things.

ⓒ Leonardo da Vinci did many different jobs well.

ⓓ The *Mona Lisa* was painted by Leonardo da Vinci.

Organizing

Complete the chart.

Leonardo's Jobs	Leonardo's Actions
painter	painted the _____
_____	learned a lot about the human body
inventor	invented _____ like cannons and guns
_____	_____ a helicopter and an airplane

Vocabulary

Fill in the blanks.

> take place   complete   sculpture   invent   weapon   cannon

1. The birthday party will _____ on Saturday night.

2. The pirates fired their _____ at the other ship.

3. That _____ looks like a horse.

4. The soldier always carries his _____ with him.

5. John is good at teaching and loves students. He's a _____ teacher.

6. He is trying to _____ a time machine.

Summary 25

Listen to the summary and fill in the blanks.

The Renaissance _____ in the past. Leonardo da Vinci was a Renaissance man.

He had many different _____. He _____ the *Mona Lisa*. He also made

many _____. He _____ lots of different things. He invented weapons like

_____. He also designed a helicopter and an airplane.

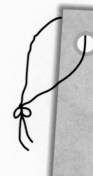

Tip One-Minute Grammar!

Use **too** and **either** to mean "also." But use **too** in positive sentences and use **either** in negative sentences.

He was a writer and scientist **too**.
Kare doesn't like bats **either**.

Rachel's Busy Day

Read and check.

	True	False
1. A chef works at a restaurant.	☐	☐
2. Meals have different ingredients in them.	☐	☐
3. A waiter cooks food.	☐	☐

New Words 🔊 26

Listen and repeat.

1 shrimp:

2 throw away:

3 assist: to help

4 satisfied: pleased

5 supply: an amount of something

6 complain: to say something is bad

New Sentences

Write a, b, or c.

a  **b**  **c**

1 ☐ Her junior chef assists her.

2 ☐ He has to throw it away.

3 ☐ She checks on the food supply.

Rachel's Busy Day

Rachel is a busy woman. She's the head chef at Primo's, a popular Italian restaurant. It opens at five, but she arrives there at noon. First, she decides on the day's special: shrimp and pasta in a cream sauce. Then she checks on the food supply. She needs more shrimp and pasta, so she orders them.

Around four o'clock, Rachel starts preparing the soups, and her three junior chefs assist her. At five, customers start ordering meals. Suddenly, everyone is really busy. One chef burns the chicken. He has to throw away the chicken. One customer complains. He isn't satisfied with his meal. So Rachel gives him a bottle of wine to make him pleased.

At ten o'clock, the restaurant is closed. The junior chefs clean up the kitchen while Rachel plans tomorrow's menu. She's tired but happy that things have gone well.

Listening Quiz! ● 28
1 ⓐ Yes   ⓑ No
2 ⓐ at ten   ⓑ at eleven

Choose or write the answer.

1 Rachel decides on the day's special: shrimp and _____ in a cream sauce.

ⓐ chicken ⓑ wine ⓒ vegetables ⓓ pasta

2 One _____ isn't satisfied with his meal.

ⓐ chef ⓑ customer ⓒ waiter ⓓ woman

3 What time does the restaurant open?

ⓐ twelve ⓑ four ⓒ five ⓓ ten

4 What does Rachel give to the unsatisfied customer?

- She gives him a bottle of _____ .

Main Idea

Choose the main idea.

ⓐ There are three junior chefs working at the restaurant.

ⓑ Rachel is busy working at her restaurant all day long.

ⓒ Rachel orders some food for the restaurant.

ⓓ The restaurant opens at five o'clock.

Organizing

Complete the chart.

Rachel's Day

at noon	_____ at the restaurant
around four o'clock	starts preparing the _____
at ten o'clock	_____ tomorrow's menu

Fill in the blanks.

> shrimp   supply   assist   throw away   satisfied   complain

1. The school has a big _____ of pens and pencils.
2. Don't _____ that newspaper. I want to read it.
3. Are you _____ with your grade? You did very well.
4. My brother loves to eat _____ cocktail.
5. You _____ too much. Try to be happier.
6. Can you _____ me? I need some help.

Summary 29

Listen to the summary and fill in the blanks.

Rachel arrives at Primo's at _____ and starts working. She _____ the

day's special and orders some _____. Her junior chefs _____ her. One

chef burns some chicken. One customer _____ about the meal. Finally,

the day ends. The junior chefs _____ the kitchen, and Rachel prepares for

tomorrow.

Tip One-Minute Grammar!

Prepositions of time are used to talk about when something happens.

It opens **at** five. [at + clock time]
They go to school **on** Monday. [on + day/date]
Her birthday is **in** July. [in + month/year]

Jobs of the Future

Read and check.

	True	False
1. People make money from their jobs.	☐	☐
2. Some people work on the moon now.	☐	☐
3. There will be no jobs in the future.	☐	☐

New Words 30

Listen and repeat.

1. **space:**

2. **advanced:** developed

3. **technology:** knowledge of science

4. **tourism:** the travel business

5. **industry:** a kind of business

6. **society:** a large group of people in a country

New Sentences

Write a, b, or c.

   a

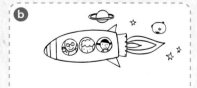   b

   c

1. ☐ There will be many jobs using technology.

2. ☐ Humans may start traveling in space.

3. ☐ There will be lots of jobs in the tourism industry.

Jobs of the Future

- Topic: Future Jobs
- Genre: Nonfiction

As the world changes, people's jobs also change. Some of them disappear, so no one does them. For instance, some people used to deliver ice. But these days, it's not easy to see the 'iceman.' Instead, there will be new jobs, perhaps more jobs in the future. People are getting older, so there will be many jobs in health care. People have more free time and they would take vacations more often. This means there will be lots of new jobs in the tourism industry.

Every year, our society gets more advanced. So there will be many jobs using technology. People will have to study for a long time before they can do them. And soon, humans may start traveling in space. There will be jobs on the moon in the future. Maybe you can become a spaceship cleaner on the moon!

Listening Quiz! 32

1 ⓐ Yes   ⓑ No
2 ⓐ ice   ⓑ spaceship

Details

Choose or write the answer.

1 As the world changes, people's jobs also _____ .

ⓐ change   ⓑ disappear   ⓒ deliver   ⓓ study

2 Every year, our _____ gets more advanced.

ⓐ society   ⓑ moon   ⓒ future   ⓓ health care

3 What is a job that people can't see easily today?

ⓐ doctor   ⓑ teacher   ⓒ iceman   ⓓ spaceship cleaner

4 Where will there be jobs in the future?

- There will be jobs on the _____ in the future.

Main Idea

Choose the main idea.

ⓐ There will be many kinds of new jobs in the future.

ⓑ Lots of jobs are available in the tourism industry.

ⓒ Some people will work on the moon in the future.

ⓓ A few people work in health care today.

Organizing

Complete the chart.

Cause		Effect
• People are getting older.	→	• There will be jobs in _____ care.
• People have more free time.	→	• There will be jobs in the _____ industry.
• Society gets more advanced.	→	• There will be jobs using _____ .

Vocabulary

Fill in the blanks.

> tourism   industry   society   advanced   technology   space

1. There is no air in outer _____ .

2. He comes from a very traditional _____ .

3. Travel agents and tour guides work in the _____ industry.

4. We have the _____ to send a man to Mars today.

5. Lasers are one kind of _____ technology.

6. One _____ that is very important is the automobile industry.

Summary 33

Listen to the summary and fill in the blanks.

Some jobs disappear when _____ improves. For example, there are few _____ today. There will be many kinds of jobs in the _____ . Health care jobs will be important. So will the _____ industry. Since technology is becoming more _____ , people may work in outer _____ in the future, too.

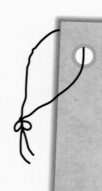

Tip One-Minute Grammar!

Use **there will be** as the future tense of "there is/are"

There will be different jobs in the future.
There will be many jobs in health care.

The Miser and His Gold

Read and check.

	True	False
1. Misers hate money.	☐	☐
2. Gold is valuable.	☐	☐
3. A thief gives money to other people.	☐	☐

New Words 34

Listen and repeat.

1 bury:

2 coin:

3 lock:

4 alone: with no one

5 miser: a greedy person

6 overhear: to hear what other people are saying without knowledge

New Sentences

Write a, b, or c.

a    **b**    **c**

1 ☐ He buried it in his backyard.

2 ☐ He had hundreds of gold coins.

3 ☐ He locked his gold in a box.

The Miser and His Gold

• Topic: Miser
• Genre: Aesop's Fables

An old miser once lived alone. He didn't have a wife, children, or any friends. However, he had hundreds of gold coins. But he never spent his money. Instead, he locked his gold in a box and buried it in his backyard.

Every Friday, the miser went to his backyard and dug up the box of coins. He said, "It's my gold! It's all mine, mine, mine!" He did this at night, so his neighbors couldn't see anything. However, one night, the miser was speaking too loudly, so a thief walking outside overheard him. The thief waited until the miser went to bed. Then he climbed the fence, dug up the box, and took the gold.

The next Friday, the miser went to see his money. He saw a huge hole in the ground. "Oh, no!" he cried, "Someone has stolen my money!"

Listening Quiz! 🔘 36

1 ⓐ Yes   ⓑ No

2 ⓐ his front yard   ⓑ his backya

Details

Choose or write the answer.

1 Every Friday, the miser went to his backyard and _____ the box of coins.

ⓐ dug up   ⓑ buried   ⓒ climbed   ⓓ locked

2 The thief waited until the miser went to _____.

ⓐ work   ⓑ the store   ⓒ school   ⓓ bed

3 What did the miser see in the ground the next Friday?

ⓐ a box   ⓑ a huge hole   ⓒ gold coins   ⓓ a thief

4 How did the thief get into the miser's backyard?

- He climbed the _____.

Main Idea

Choose the main idea.

ⓐ A thief stole all of a miser's gold from his backyard.

ⓑ A miser kept his gold coins in a box.

ⓒ There were hundreds of gold coins buried in the ground.

ⓓ The thief gave the miser back all of his money.

Organizing

Complete the chart.

A miser buried all of his gold _____ in a box in his _____.

⬇

Every _____, the miser dug up his box of coins.

⬇

A _____ stole all of the miser's coins while he was sleeping.

Vocabulary

Fill in the blanks.

> miser   coin   lock   bury   overheard   alone

1 I need one more _____ to put into the vending machine.

2 I _____ him saying that he didn't like me.

3 Please _____ the door when you leave the house.

4 I went to the theater _____ because all of my friends were busy.

5 That _____ won't even give his children any money!

6 Did the dog _____ the bone in the garden?

Summary 37

Listen to the summary and fill in the blanks.

A _____ buried his _____ coins in a box in his backyard. Every Friday, he

_____ up his coins to look at them. One night, a thief _____ the miser

speaking. The miser went to bed. Then, the thief dug up the _____ and

_____ them.

(Tip) One-Minute Grammar!

Possessive pronouns are words like **mine**, **yours**, **his**, **hers**, **ours**, and **theirs**. Use them to show possession.

It's my gold. ⟶ It's **mine**.
That's her cap. ⟶ That's **hers**.

Who Donated the Money?

Read and check.

	True	False
1. Some people give money to poor people.	☐	☐
2. People give presents on Christmas.	☐	☐
3. People with houses live at homeless center.	☐	☐

New Words 38

Listen and repeat.

1 receive:

2 anonymous: unnamed

3 lose: not to have anymore

4 financial: relating to money

5 homeless: not having a house

6 donation: giving something to help others

New Sentences

Write a, b, or c.

a
b
c

1 ☐ They remain anonymous.

2 ☐ One family had some financial problems.

3 ☐ They receive donations from others.

Who Donated the Money?

Sometimes people don't have enough money. Maybe they lost their jobs or had to spend lots of money at the hospital. In these cases, they often receive donations from others. Many donors prefer to remain anonymous. This means nobody knows their names.

Last year, around Christmas, one family had some financial problems. They couldn't buy any presents for their children. But, on Christmas Day, they got a phone call. The person just said, "Look outside." In front of their house were two big bags of presents. Who gave them the presents? No one knows.

A few years ago, there were many people at a homeless center. Suddenly, a man drove up in his car. He was dressed like Santa Claus. He gave $100 to each person there. There were over 350 people at the center. What was the man's name? No one knows.

Listening Quiz! 40

1 ⓐ Yes   ⓑ No

2 ⓐ food   ⓑ presents

Choose or write the answer.

1 Many _____ prefer to remain anonymous.

ⓐ jobs   ⓑ donors   ⓒ presents   ⓓ centers

2 People who don't have money often _____ donations from others.

ⓐ lose   ⓑ spend   ⓒ receive   ⓓ give

3 The man dressed like _____ gave $100 to each person at the homeless center.

ⓐ a ghost   ⓑ the Easter Bunny   ⓒ Santa Claus   ⓓ a vampire

4 How many people were at the homeless center that Santa Claus visited?

- There were over _____ people at the center.

Main Idea

Choose the main idea.

ⓐ Santa Claus gave everyone $100 on Christmas.

ⓑ One family got lots of free presents.

ⓒ Some people lose their jobs sometimes.

ⓓ People often donate anonymously.

Organizing

Complete the chart.

To Whom?	What was donated?
one family with _____ problems	two big bags of _____
people at a _____ center	_____ to each person

Vocabulary

Fill in the blanks.

> lose   receive   anonymous   financial   homeless   donation

1. I want to _____ an MP3 player on my birthday.

2. The _____ man sleeps under the bridge every night.

3. Be careful not to _____ your watch. It costs a lot of money.

4. Peter will make a _____ of $1,000 to the charity.

5. The company is having some _____ problems now.

6. An _____ person wrote the letter. No one signed it.

Summary 41

Listen to the summary and fill in the blanks.

Some people have _____ problems. But some _____ people often help

them out. Last Christmas, one family had no money. But someone _____ two

bags of _____ to them. Another year, a man _____ like Santa Claus

visited a _____ center. He gave everyone there $100.

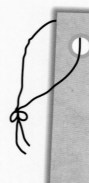

Tip One-Minute Grammar!

Use question words to ask questions. Some question words are **who**, **what**, **when**, **where**, **how**, **whose**, and **why**.

> **Who** donated the money?
> **Where** did you go?

The World's Richest Man

Read and check.

	True	False
1. A rich person has no money.	☐	☐
2. A worker works for a company.	☐	☐
3. People at companies have meetings.	☐	☐

New Words 42

Listen and repeat.

1 electronics:

2 wealthy: rich

3 employee: a worker

4 own: to have

5 salary: money a person earns for regular work

6 share: to use something with others

New Sentences

Write a, b, or c.

a    **b**    **c**

1 ☐ He owned an electronics company.

2 ☐ He started sharing his money with everyone.

3 ☐ There was a wealthy man.

The World's Richest Man

There was once a wealthy man named John Dollar. He owned an electronics company. He loved money, so he worked and worked every day. He also made his employees work very hard. John became richer and richer. Soon, he was the richest man in the world. One day, John was walking through his company. "You there," he said to a worker. "Why aren't the employees smiling? What's wrong with everyone?" he asked. The worker answered, "We're tired because we never get any breaks. We work hard, but we're still very poor." John went home and thought about what the worker said. The next day, he called a meeting. "I have enough money," he said. "Now I want everyone to be happy." John gave his employees the day off. Then he raised their salaries. He started sharing his money with everyone. And the workers at his company became happier and happier.

Listening Quiz! ● 44

1 ⓐ Yes   ⓑ No

2 ⓐ electronics ⓑ automobile

Choose or write the answer.

1 John Dollar _____ an electronics company.

ⓐ worked   ⓑ owned   ⓒ shared   ⓓ visited

2 John gave his _____ the day off.

ⓐ company   ⓑ electronics   ⓒ owner   ⓓ employees

3 What did John Dollar raise?

ⓐ salaries   ⓑ the company   ⓒ the employees   ⓓ the workers

4 Why were the employees tired?

- Because they never got any _____ .

Main Idea

Choose the main idea.

ⓐ John Dollar was the world's richest man.

ⓑ The employees were tired and poor.

ⓒ John Dollar had a meeting at his company.

ⓓ John Dollar learned to share with others.

Organizing

Complete the chart.

> John Dollar became the _____ man in the world.

⬇

> His employees weren't _____ since they were tired and poor.

⬇

> John started _____ his money with everyone at the company.

Vocabulary

Fill in the blanks.

> own   wealthy   electronics   employee   salary   share

1. Don't take that bag. You don't _____ it!
2. Her father is an _____ at a big company.
3. A millionaire is a very _____ person.
4. Children often don't like to _____ things with others.
5. He earns a big _____, so he has a lot of money.
6. TVs, DVD players, and computers are all kinds of _____.

Summary 45

Listen to the summary and fill in the blanks.

John Dollar owned an _____ company. He became the world's richest man.

He noticed that his _____ were not smiling. One said that they were

_____ and tired. So John decided to _____ his money with them. He

gave them time off and _____ their _____, too.

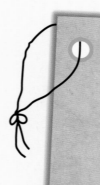

Tip One-Minute Grammar!

Use **make** to show how a person forces another to do something.
make + object + verb

He **made** his employees work hard.
Our teacher **makes** us study every day.

The History of Money

Before You Read

Read and check.

	True	False
1. People buy things with money.	☐	☐
2. People use gold coins today.	☐	☐
3. People will use animals for money in the future.	☐	☐

New Words 46

Listen and repeat.

① **firewood:**

② **carry:** to bring

③ **check:** paper money substitute

④ **metal:** a solid object like steel, silver, or gold

⑤ **trade:** to exchange one thing for another

⑥ **melt:** to heat something until it becomes a liquid

New Sentences

Write a, b, or c.

a	b	c

① ☐ People learned how to melt metal to make coins.

② ☐ He traded four apples for three oranges.

③ ☐ People use checks and credit cards.

The History of Money

A long time ago, there was no money. Then people bartered goods. That means they traded with each other. Maybe a person traded four apples for three oranges. Or another person traded shoes for firewood. Later, people used animals for money. They bought items with cows, pigs, horses, and chickens. And in some cultures, people used shells as money. In fact, some places in Africa still use them today.

People then learned how to melt metal. So they could make coins. They made coins from gold, silver, copper, and other metals. Gold and silver coins were popular for hundreds of years. Later, some countries began to use paper money.

These days, we use both coins and paper money. But people also use checks and credit cards. They can buy things with no money. So some people don't even carry money now!

Listening Quiz! 48

1 ⓐ Yes   ⓑ No

2 ⓐ animals   ⓑ credit cards

Details

Choose or write the answer.

1 Some places in _____ still use shells as money today.

ⓐ America   ⓑ Asia   ⓒ Africa   ⓓ Australia

2 People made coins from gold, silver, copper, and other _____.

ⓐ papers   ⓑ shells   ⓒ metals   ⓓ animals

3 What kind of money did countries use after making coins?

ⓐ checks   ⓑ paper money   ⓒ seashells   ⓓ credit cards

4 What does barter mean?

- It means people _____ with each other.

Main Idea

Choose the main idea.

ⓐ Most people use credit cards or checks these days.

ⓑ Bartering was an early form of trade.

ⓒ People have used many different forms of money.

ⓓ Some Africans still use shells as money.

Organizing

Complete the chart.

The History of Money

bartering → trading _____ or shells → _____

_____ and credit cards ← paper money ←

Vocabulary

Fill in the blanks.

> trade   firewood   melt   metal   check   carry

1 Can you _____ this box for me? I'm not strong enough.

2 Winter is coming. We need to cut some more _____.

3 Steel is a very strong _____ that people use to make buildings.

4 Will you _____ your sandwich for my cookies?

5 Should I pay with cash or a _____?

6 When you _____ butter quickly, you need heat.

Summary   49

Listen to the summary and fill in the blanks.

Throughout history, people have used many forms of _____. At first, people

bartered goods. Then they _____ animals or shells. Later, they learned to

_____ metal. So they made gold and _____ coins. Today, people use

paper money, checks, and _____ cards. Some people don't even _____

money now.

Tip One-Minute Grammar!

Use **how to+verb** to talk about the way to do something. You can use it to talk about a skill or ability.

People learned **how to** melt metal.
My sister knows **how to** play the flute.

The Little Prince

Read and check.

	True	False
1. A prince is the daughter of a king.	☐	☐
2. People live on Earth.	☐	☐
3. Roses can speak in real world.	☐	☐

New Words 50

Listen and repeat.

1 **desert:**

2 **odd:** strange

3 **bite:** to use the teeth to cut into something

4 **lie:** to say something false

5 **encounter:** to meet

6 **planet:** a large, round object in space that moves around a star

New Sentences

Write a, b, or c.

 **a**

 **b**

 **c**

1 ☐ A little prince lived on a planet.

2 ☐ The snake bit the prince.

3 ☐ The prince encountered a businessman.

The Little Prince

A little prince once lived on a planet. One day, a rose started growing there. The prince loved his rose, but she lied to him once. So he decided to leave and visit other planets.

While visiting other planets, the prince met some strange people on them. On the first planet, he met a king. On another planet, he met a drunk. He also encountered a businessman and a lamplighter. The prince thought all of them were odd.

Then the prince arrived on Earth and landed in the desert. After some time, he became lonely and wanted to see his rose again. A snake told the prince it could send him back to his planet. And the snake bit the prince, who died. Then the prince and his rose were together again.

Listening Quiz! 52

1 ⓐ Yes   ⓑ No

2 ⓐ a rose   ⓑ a snake

Details

Choose or write the answer.

1 On the first planet, the little prince met a _____.

    ⓐ king   ⓑ businessman   ⓒ rose   ⓓ drunk

2 The prince became _____ and wanted to see his rose again.

    ⓐ angry   ⓑ odd   ⓒ satisfied   ⓓ lonely

3 Why did the little prince leave his rose?

    ⓐ She was mean.   ⓑ She lied to him.   ⓒ She died.   ⓓ He didn't like her.

4 What happened after the little prince died?

    - The little prince and his rose were _____ again.

Main Idea

Choose the main idea.

    ⓐ The little prince visited many places and then went back to his planet.

    ⓑ A snake bit the little prince and killed him.

    ⓒ The little prince met a king on one of the planets.

    ⓓ The rose lied to the little prince, so he left his planet.

Organizing

Complete the chart.

> The little prince lived with a _____ on his planet.

⬇

> On other planets, he met a king, a _____, a businessman, and a _____.

⬇

> He went back to his planet after he met a _____ on Earth.

Vocabulary

Fill in the blanks.

> odd   lie   encounter   planet   desert   bite

1 Don't _____ to me. You should always tell the truth.

2 That's _____. I put my keys here, but now they are gone.

3 A _____ gets very little rain all year long.

4 We live on the _____ called Earth.

5 That cat will _____ you if you are not careful.

6 We will _____ many people on our trip to the city.

Summary 53

Listen to the summary and fill in the blanks.

The little _____ lived with a rose. His rose _____ to him, so he left his

planet. He _____ many people while traveling. He landed in a _____ on

Earth. But he became _____ and missed his rose. A snake _____ him, he

died, and then he met his rose again.

Tip One-Minute Grammar!

Use **and** to combine two actions into one sentence.

He decided to leave.
+
He decided to visit other planets.

→ He decided to leave **and** visit other planets.

Aliens in Stories and Movies

Before You Read

Read and check.

	True	False
1. Aliens are from Earth.	☐	☐
2. Aliens in movies can be unfriendly.	☐	☐
3. Aliens have attacked Earth in real world.	☐	☐

New Words 🔊 54

Listen and repeat.

1 alien:

2 mean: unfriendly

3 destroy: to end

4 murder: to kill a person

5 monstrous: like a monster

6 fiction: stories about imaginary people and events

New Sentences

Write a, b, or c.

1 ☐ The alien attacks and murders humans.

2 ☐ In movies, aliens are often mean.

3 ☐ The aliens tried to destroy Earth.

Aliens in Stories and Movies

• Topic: Aliens
• Genre: Nonfiction

Are we alone? Many people have looked at the stars and wondered that. No one knows if there are aliens or not. But writers and filmmakers often imagine aliens. In fact, in fiction, there are many different kinds of aliens.

In lots of stories, the aliens are unfriendly. They often visit Earth to attack and murder humans. This happened in H.G. Well's *The War of the Worlds*. Martians came to Earth and killed many people. In the end though, all of the aliens died. Also, in movies, aliens are often mean. The creature in *Alien* was a monstrous alien. The aliens in *Independence Day* tried to destroy Earth.

But there are also good aliens. Sometimes, like in *E.T.*, they just visited Earth. They seemed curious and friendly to humans. Even more the alien in *E.T.* learned to speak English by repeating what humans say.

Listening Quiz! ● 56
1 ⓐ Yes   ⓑ No
2 ⓐ Earth   ⓑ another planet

Choose or write the answer.

1. In _____, there are many different kinds of aliens.
   ⓐ the stars   ⓑ Earth   ⓒ writers   ⓓ fiction

2. The creature in *Alien* was a _____ alien.
   ⓐ friendly   ⓑ kind   ⓒ beautiful   ⓓ monstrous

3. Which movie had good aliens in it?
   ⓐ *Independence Day*   ⓑ *The War of the Worlds*   ⓒ *E.T.*   ⓓ *Alien*

4. What happened in *The War of the Worlds*?
   - Martians came to Earth and _____ many people.

Main Idea

Choose the main idea.

ⓐ There were Martians in *The War of the Worlds*.
ⓑ Some filmmakers make movies about aliens.
ⓒ The aliens in *E.T.* were friendly.
ⓓ Books and movies have both good and bad aliens.

Organizing

Complete the chart.

Title	What the Aliens Did
The War of the Worlds	_____ came to Earth and killed many people.
_____	The aliens tried to destroy Earth.
E.T.	The alien learned to _____ English.

Vocabulary

Fill in the blanks.

> alien   murder   fiction   mean   monstrous   destroy

1 You shouldn't hit people. Stop being so _____!

2 The bomb will _____ the building in a few minutes.

3 A dragon is a fire-breathing _____ animal that is very dangerous.

4 I prefer to read _____ books to nonfiction books.

5 The _____ visited Earth on its spaceship.

6 The criminal tried to _____ the young boy.

Summary 57

Listen to the summary and fill in the blanks.

No one knows if there are _____. But writers and filmmakers often _____ them. Sometimes the aliens are _____. In *The War of the Worlds* and *Independence Day*, aliens killed many _____. They were _____ aliens and tried to _____ Earth. But some aliens, like in *E.T.* are good.

(Tip) One-Minute Grammar!

Use **no one** to mean nobody. Use it to talk about when there are zero people somewhere or doing something.

No one knows if there are aliens or not.
No one answered the phone.

A Visit to Mars

Before You Read

Read and check.

	True	False
1. Humans live on Mars.	☐	☐
2. Humans have two heads.	☐	☐
3. Spaceships can travel to other planets.	☐	☐

New Words 🔊 58

Listen and repeat.

1 **Mars:**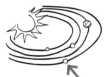

2 **astronaut:**

3 **peace:** no fighting or war

4 **communicate:** to speak with

5 **translate:** to change from one language to another

6 **land:** to come down to the ground

New Sentences

Write a, b, or c.

1 ☐ The three astronauts on *Eagle 1* were excited.

2 ☐ The computer can communicate with Martians.

3 ☐ They landed on Mars.

A Visit to Mars

"We're about to land on Mars!" said Tina, the head astronaut. The three astronauts on *Eagle 1* were excited since they were the first people to visit the planet. "Look, there are Martians down there," said Lewis. There were several tiny green people below. They had three arms, four legs, and two heads each! "I hope the computer can communicate with them and translate for us," said George.

They landed on Mars and opened the doors of the spaceship. The Martians looked at them and started making funny noises. "What are they saying?" said Tina. The computer answered, "They think you look silly because you only have one head."

"We are from Earth. We come in peace," said Tina. The Martian leader smiled at them. "Even though you have one head, you seem like good people," he answered. Then Earthlings and Martians became great friends.

Listening Quiz! 🔘 60

1 ⓐ Yes   ⓑ No

2 ⓐ Martians   ⓑ Earthlings

Details

Choose or write the answer.

1 The Martians had three arms, four _____, and two heads each.

ⓐ legs ⓑ eyes ⓒ fingers ⓓ shoulders

2 The three astronauts were _____ since they were the first people to visit the planet.

ⓐ silly ⓑ bored ⓒ excited ⓓ upset

3 Who translated for the astronauts?

ⓐ the Martians ⓑ the Earthlings ⓒ the computer ⓓ *Eagle 1*

4 Why did the Martians think the astronauts looked silly?

- Because they only had one _____.

Main Idea

Choose the main idea.

ⓐ Some astronauts landed on Mars and met some Martians.

ⓑ The Martians had three arms, four legs, and two heads.

ⓒ The computer translated for the astronauts.

ⓓ The astronauts rode on *Eagle 1* all the way to Mars.

Organizing

Complete the chart.

Some astronauts met some Martians on _____.

⬇

The computer _____ the Martian language for the astronauts.

⬇

Earthlings and Martians became _____ with each other.

Vocabulary

Fill in the blanks.

> communicate   astronaut   Mars   land   translate   peace

1. We learn languages to _____ with people from other countries.

2. A Martian is an alien that comes from _____.

3. The countries stopped fighting, so there was finally _____.

4. The _____ will spend one week in space at the space station.

5. Sumi can _____ from Korean to English.

6. The helicopter is going to _____ on top of the building.

Summary 61

Listen to the summary and fill in the blanks.

Three astronauts flew a _____ to Mars. They saw some _____ waiting

for them. They used the _____ to _____ with the Martians. The Martians

thought they looked _____ since they only had one head. The Earthlings

wanted _____. So they all became friends.

Tip One-Minute Grammar!

Put two or more adjectives in front of a noun to describe it. The order for adjectives is: **size + shape + color**.

There were **tiny green** people below.
Look at the **big round pink** ball.

Apollo 11

Read and check.

	True	False
1. Some people have visited the moon.	☐	☐
2. The moon is bigger than Earth.	☐	☐
3. A spaceship can fly under water.	☐	☐

New Words 62

Listen and repeat.

1 **amazing:** incredible

2 **reach:** to arrive

3 **act:** an event

4 **launch:** to send into space

5 **hero:** a person who does something great

6 **satellite:** an object sent into space to travel around the earth, or another planet

New Sentences

Write a, b, or c.

1 ☐ **The United States launched** *Apollo 11.*

2 ☐ **The astronauts were all heroes!**

3 ☐ **They sent satellites into space.**

Apollo 11

photo © NASA

photo © NASA

In 1957, the Soviet Union sent a satellite into space. Then, the USA and Soviet Union began the space race. First, they sent satellites into space. Then, they sent animals and people there. Finally, they tried sending men to the moon.

In the 1960s, the United States worked hard on the space program. It spent very much money on it. On July 16, 1969, it launched *Apollo 11*. There were three men in the spaceship. It took them four days to reach the moon. Then, on July 20, *Apollo 11* landed on the moon. Neil Armstrong became the first man to set foot on it. Another astronaut, Buzz Aldrin, walked on the moon with him. On Earth, millions of people watched the moon landing. It was an amazing act. A few days later, on July 24, the astronauts returned to Earth. They were all heroes!

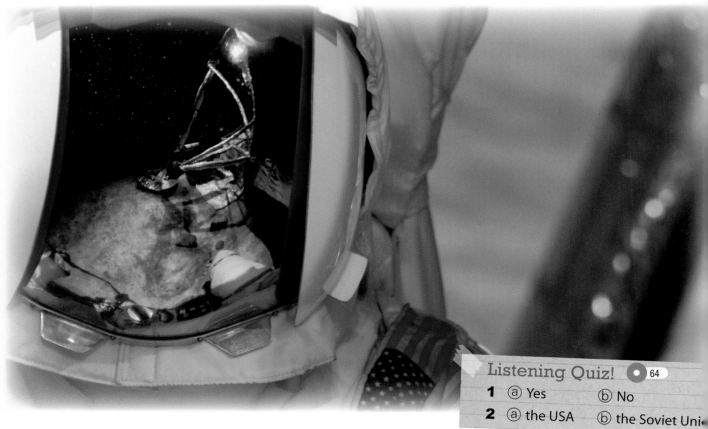

Listening Quiz! ● 64
1 ⓐ Yes   ⓑ No
2 ⓐ the USA   ⓑ the Soviet Uni

Details

Choose or write the answer.

1 In the 1960s, the United States worked hard on the _____ program.

ⓐ satellite   ⓑ space   ⓒ moon   ⓓ star

2 It took them four days to reach the _____.

ⓐ moon   ⓑ Mars   ⓒ Earth   ⓓ planet

3 When did the astronauts first walk on the moon?

ⓐ July 2, 1969   ⓑ July 16, 1969   ⓒ July 20, 1969   ⓓ July 24, 1969

4 What happened after the Soviet Union sent a satellite into space?

- The USA and Soviet Union began the _____ _____.

Main Idea

Choose the main idea.

ⓐ The USA and Soviet Union both launched satellites.

ⓑ The space race lasted for many years.

ⓒ Neil Armstrong was an astronaut on *Apollo 11*.

ⓓ The USA succeeded to send men to the moon in 1969.

Organizing

Complete the chart.

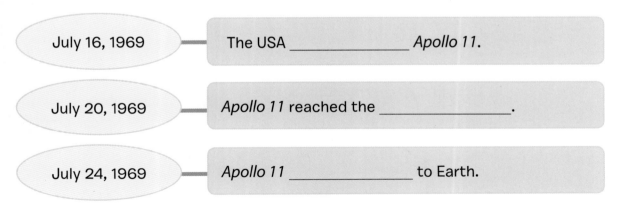

July 16, 1969 — The USA _____ *Apollo 11*.

July 20, 1969 — *Apollo 11* reached the _____.

July 24, 1969 — *Apollo 11* _____ to Earth.

Vocabulary

Fill in the blanks.

> satellite   launch   reach   act   amazing   hero

1 That's _____ ! I can't believe how well you play the piano.

2 They are going to _____ the rocket tomorrow morning.

3 You saved that baby from the fire. You're a _____ !

4 What time are we going to _____ the train station?

5 The _____ is thousands of miles above Earth.

6 His first _____ as a president was to declare a holiday.

Summary   65

Listen to the summary and fill in the blanks.

After the Soviet Union launched a _____ in 1957, it and the USA began the

space race. Both countries tried to _____ the moon first. In 1969, the USA

_____ *Apollo 11*. On July 20, 1969, Neil Armstrong _____ on the moon.

He and the other two _____ were _____ .

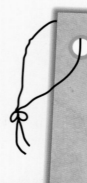

Tip One-Minute Grammar!

Use prepositions of movement to show the direction something is going. Some of them are **into**, **out of**, **through**, and **around**.

The Soviet Union sent a satellite **into** space.
You should walk **around** the corner.

Vocabulary Index

Unit 1
crew
discover
hire
inn
pirate
possession

Unit 2
attract
creature
fascinating
fin
pressure
stretch

Unit 3
bottom
crab
disappear
escape
jaw
shadow

Unit 4
area
lay
nutrient
predator
provide
shallow

Unit 5
continue
curious
dawn
elf
stitch
workshop

Unit 6
cannon
complete
invent
sculpture
take place
weapon

Unit 7
assist
complain
satisfied
shrimp
supply
throw away

Unit 8
advanced
industry
society
space
technology
tourism

Vocabulary Index

evelop Reading skills with Vocabulary, Listening, Writing plus Grammar

Reading Plus 3

WORKBOOK

Clue & Key

Treasure Island

A Write the meaning of the word in your mother language. Then write the words.

1 crew _____ _____

2 discover _____ _____

3 hire _____ _____

4 inn _____ _____

5 pirate _____ _____

6 possession _____ _____

B Choose the meaning for each underlined word.

1 Jim <u>discovers</u> they are pirates.

    ⓐ finds out   ⓑ forgets   ⓒ opens

2 Jim goes through the man's <u>possessions</u>.

    ⓐ pockets   ⓑ maps   ⓒ belongings

C Fill in the blanks.

hire	inn	pirates

1 Jim is working at his family's _____.

2 Jim and his friends _____ some crews.

3 Jim and the others have battles with the _____.

D Unscramble the sentences.

1 get / they / the island / to / .

…▸ _____

2 man / mysterious / a / arrives / .

…▸ _____

3 the island / they / to / sail / .

…▸ _____

4 the treasure / they / to find / plan / .

…▸ _____

5 rich men / as / sail back / they / home / .

…▸ _____

E Complete the sentences. Use 'when.' *Grammar*

1 I am sleeping _____. (Mom comes in)

2 She was thirty _____. (she had her baby)

3 They are playing a game _____. (it begins to rain)

4 The boy is walking _____. (a dog barks at him)

5 He is taking a shower _____. (the telephone rings)

6 I went there _____. (I was a child)

F Translate each sentence into your mother language.

1 Jim Hawkins is working at his family's inn when a mysterious man arrives.

...▶ _____

2 But that man soon dies. So Jim goes through the man's possessions and finds a treasure map.

...▶ _____

3 Jim and his friends purchase a ship, the *Hispaniola*.

...▶ _____

4 Then they hire some crews. The ship's cook is Long John Silver, a man with one leg.

...▶ _____

5 They sail to the island.

...▶ _____

6 While on the ship, Jim hears Silver talking with some other crew members.

...▶ _____

7 He discovers they are pirates.

...▶ _____

8 They plan to find the treasure, steal it, and kill Jim and his friends.

...▶ _____

9 When they get to the island, Jim and the others run away from the pirates.

...▶ _____

10 They have several battles with the pirates. In the end, the pirates lose.

...▶ _____

11 Jim and the others find the treasure.

...▶ _____

12 They leave Silver and the pirates on the island and sail back home as rich men.

...▶ _____

Creatures of the Deep

A Write the meaning of the word in your mother language. Then write the words.

❶ attract

❷ creature

❸ fascinating

❹ fin

❺ pressure

❻ stretch

B Choose the meaning for each underlined word.

❶ Many unique creatures live deep beneath the ocean.

ⓐ vegetables   ⓑ animals   ⓒ plants

❷ The gulper eel is a fascinating creature.

ⓐ strange   ⓑ scary   ⓒ interesting

C Fill in the blanks.

fins   attract   pressure

❶ Deep in the ocean, the water _____ is very high.

❷ The coelacanth looks like it has legs instead of _____.

❸ The lanternfish can make its own light to _____ other fish.

D Unscramble the sentences.

1 light / there / no / is / .

...▶ _____

2 usually / teeth / have / they / sharp / .

...▶ _____

3 eyes / some / huge / have / .

...▶ _____

4 deep / thousands of meters / is / the ocean / .

...▶ _____

5 live deep / viper fish / the ocean / in / .

...▶ _____

E Rewrite the sentences. Use 'used to.' Grammar

1 They don't live in Seoul anymore.

...▶ _____

2 I don't play soccer anymore.

...▶ _____

3 Mark doesn't study hard anymore.

...▶ _____

4 My parents don't work at a company anymore.

...▶ _____

5 We don't go to kindergarten anymore.

...▶ _____

6 She doesn't have a cat anymore.

...▶ _____

F Translate each sentence into your mother language.

1 In some places, the ocean is thousands of meters deep.

> ⋯▶ _____

2 Deep in the ocean, there's no light, and the water pressure is very high.

> ⋯▶ _____

3 Scientists used to think nothing lived there. But, in fact, many unique creatures live deep beneath the ocean.

> ⋯▶ _____

4 Viper fish live deep in the ocean.

> ⋯▶ _____

5 Some have huge eyes, and others can make their own light. They usually have long, sharp teeth.

> ⋯▶ _____

6 The gulper eel is another fascinating deep-sea creature.

> ⋯▶ _____

7 It has a stomach that can stretch so far that it can eat fish even bigger than it is!

> ⋯▶ _____

8 Like the viper fish, the lanternfish can make its own light.

> ⋯▶ _____

9 It does that to attract other fish to catch and eat them.

> ⋯▶ _____

10 The coelacanth lives deep under water, too.

> ⋯▶ _____

11 It even looks like it has legs instead of fins. How unique!

> ⋯▶ _____

Shark Attack!

A Write the meaning of the word in your mother language. Then write the words.

1 bottom

_____

2 crab

_____

3 disappear

_____

4 escape

_____

5 jaw

_____

6 shadow

_____

B Choose the meaning for each underlined word.

1 Rick and Sharon <u>escaped</u> and swam up to the boat.

   ⓐ got through   ⓑ got away   ⓒ got along

2 Suddenly, all the fish <u>disappeared</u>.

   ⓐ went away   ⓑ went together   ⓒ went back

C Fill in the blanks.

> jaws   bottom   shadow

1 The shark opened its _____.

2 There was a big _____ above them.

3 They swam down to the _____.

D Unscramble the sentences.

1 looks / water / great / the / .

...▶ _____

2 into / dived / the / Rick and Sharon / water / .

...▶ _____

3 the shark / circling / was / around them / .

...▶ _____

4 was / and closer / it / getting / closer / .

...▶ _____

5 you / scuba diving / ready / to go / are / ?

...▶ _____

E Fill in the blanks. Use the past continuous tense. *Grammar*

1 I (eat) _____ dinner last night.

2 Chris (talk) _____ to Deanna this morning.

3 We (study) _____ science before lunch.

4 Paula (take) _____ a test at two o'clock.

5 They (fix) _____ the computer last weekend.

6 My mother and father (work) _____ at their jobs yesterday.

F Translate each sentence into your mother language.

1 "Are you ready to go scuba diving?" asked Rick.

···▶ _____

2 "Yeah, the water looks great. Let's jump in," answered Sharon.

···▶ _____

3 Rick and Sharon dived into the water. They swam down to the bottom.

···▶ _____

4 There were all kinds of fish in the ocean.

···▶ _____

5 They saw colorful fish, big and small fish, crabs, lobsters, and other sea creatures.

···▶ _____

6 Suddenly, all the fish disappeared. Rick and Sharon looked around.

···▶ _____

7 There was a big shadow above them. It was a shark! They were both scared.

···▶ _____

8 The shark was circling around them. It was getting closer and closer.

···▶ _____

9 The shark opened its jaws. It had huge teeth!

···▶ _____

10 Just then, two other big fish swam toward the shark. They were dolphins!

···▶ _____

11 They attacked the shark. They hit it with their noses.

···▶ _____

12 Rick and Sharon escaped and swam up to the boat. "I hate sharks, but I love dolphins," said Sharon.

···▶ _____

Coral Reefs

A Write the meaning of the word in your mother language. Then write the words.

1 area

2 lay

3 nutrient

4 predator

5 provide

6 shallow

B Choose the meaning for each underlined word.

1 Some <u>shallow</u> parts of the ocean have coral reefs.

    ⓐ low   ⓑ high   ⓒ wide

2 Millions of coral come together in one <u>area</u>.

    ⓐ color   ⓑ time   ⓒ place

C Fill in the blanks.

provide	nutrients	lay

1 Coral reefs _____ safe places for fish to live.

2 Many fish _____ their eggs in coral reefs.

3 The water around a reef has many _____.

D Unscramble the sentences.

1 in / are found / they / warm waters / .

···▶ _____

2 swim / sharks / the reefs / in / can't / .

···▶ _____

3 are / coral reefs / people / destroying / .

···▶ _____

4 food / coral reefs / for fish / provide / .

···▶ _____

5 will / in the ocean / be able to / more fish / live / .

···▶ _____

E Rewrite the sentences. Use 'will be able to.' Grammar

1 Jason can go to the game tomorrow.

···▶ _____

2 I can cook dinner tonight.

···▶ _____

3 They can play baseball on Saturday.

···▶ _____

4 We can study together later.

···▶ _____

5 Cindy can finish her homework tomorrow.

···▶ _____

6 I can help you next week.

···▶ _____

F Translate each sentence into your mother language.

1 Some shallow parts of the ocean have coral reefs.

···▸ _____

2 Coral looks like a hard, rocky plant. But it's actually a living creature.

···▸ _____

3 When millions of coral come together in one area, they create a coral reef.

···▸ _____

4 Coral reefs are very important for the oceans.

···▸ _____

5 First, coral reefs provide safe places for fish to live.

···▸ _____

6 Large numbers of species of fish often live in the reefs.

···▸ _____

7 Predators like sharks can't swim in the reefs.

···▸ _____

8 So the fish are safe there. For that reason, many fish lay their eggs in coral reefs.

···▸ _____

9 Coral reefs are also rich in food. They are typically found in warm waters.

···▸ _____

10 The water around a reef has many nutrients. This provides food for the fish.

···▸ _____

11 Unfortunately, people and pollution are destroying coral reefs.

···▸ _____

12 People need to take better care of the coral reefs. Then, more fish will be able to live in the ocean.

···▸ _____

The Shoemaker and the Elves

A Write the meaning of the word in your mother language. Then write the words.

1 continue

2 curious

3 dawn

4 elf

5 stitch

6 workshop

B Choose the meaning for each underlined word.

1 This <u>continued</u> for many days.

    ⓐ purchased   ⓑ kept on   ⓒ stopped

2 The shoemaker found new shoes. He was <u>curious</u> about them.

    ⓐ eager to say   ⓑ eager to write   ⓒ eager to know

C Fill in the blanks.

dawn	elves	stitched

1 An old shoemaker cut leather and _____ them together.

2 The elves made shoes all night long and left at _____.

3 Three _____ visited his workshop.

D Unscramble the sentences.

1 to bed / he / the leather / and went / cut / .

...▶ _____

2 and hid / stayed up / he / late / .

...▶ _____

3 never / the elves / again / saw / he / .

...▶ _____

4 a high price / paid / for the shoes / a customer / .

...▶ _____

5 went well / everything / him / with / .

...▶ _____

E Fill in the blanks. Use the plural of the words. Grammar

1 There are two (woman) _____ in the room.

2 Put the containers on those two (shelf) _____ .

3 We saw a family of four (deer) _____ in the forest.

4 The teacher told the (child) _____ to be quiet.

5 My brother caught three (fish) _____ at the lake.

6 There were two (wolf) _____ living in the forest.

Translate each sentence into your mother language.

1 An old shoemaker cut leather and stitched them together to make shoes every day.

...▶ _____

2 But he was still very poor. One day, he only had enough leather for one pair of shoes.

...▶ _____

3 He cut the leather and went to bed.

...▶ _____

4 In the morning, he found a brand-new pair of very well-made shoes.

...▶ _____

5 A customer came in, saw the shoes, and paid a high price for them.

...▶ _____

6 The shoemaker purchased enough leather for two pairs of shoes.

...▶ _____

7 The next day, he found two new excellent pairs of shoes.

...▶ _____

8 This continued for many days. The shoemaker was curious about the new shoes.

...▶ _____

9 So, one night, he stayed up late and hid. Around midnight, three elves visited his workshop.

...▶ _____

10 They made shoes all night long and left at dawn.

...▶ _____

11 The shoemaker never saw the elves again.

...▶ _____

12 But everything went well with him from that time.

...▶ _____

Leonardo da Vinci

A Write the meaning of the word in your mother language. Then write the words.

1 cannon

2 complete

3 invent

4 sculpture

5 take place

6 weapon

B Choose the meaning for each underlined word.

1 In the 14th century, the Renaissance <u>took place</u>.

ⓐ learned   ⓑ disappeared   ⓒ happened

2 Leonardo was a <u>complete</u> Renaissance man.

ⓐ perfect   ⓑ famous   ⓒ busy

C Fill in the blanks.

sculptures	inventor	weapons

1 He had many great ideas. He was an _____.

2 He was an artist. He made _____ and drew.

3 He invented lots of _____ like cannons and guns.

D Unscramble the sentences.

1 was / a great / he / painter /.

...▸ _____

2 new / subjects / there were / many / .

...▸ _____

3 a really / was / busy man / he /!

...▸ _____

4 learned / the / he / human body / about / .

...▸ _____

5 in the world / painted / painting / he / the most famous / .

...▸ _____

E Choose the correct words. Grammar

1 We don't play video games. We don't play computer games (too / either).

2 I can speak Korean. I can speak English (too / either).

3 Mina is tall. She is very pretty (too / either).

4 They don't go to school. They don't work (too / either).

5 Larry looks happy right now. He is smiling (too / either).

6 I can't run fast. I can't play baseball (too / either).

F Translate each sentence into your mother language.

1 In the 14th century, the Renaissance took place.

···▶ _____

2 During this time, there were so many new subjects that some people tried to study.

···▶ _____

3 People called someone who could do many jobs a "Renaissance man."

···▶ _____

4 Leonardo da Vinci was a complete Renaissance man.

···▶ _____

5 Leonardo could do many things. He was a great painter.

···▶ _____

6 He painted the *Mona Lisa*, the most famous painting in the world.

···▶ _____

7 He also made sculptures and drew. But he wasn't just an artist.

···▶ _____

8 He was a writer and scientist too. Leonardo learned a lot about the human body.

···▶ _____

9 He had many great ideas. So he was an inventor and designer as well.

···▶ _____

10 He invented lots of different weapons, like cannons and guns.

···▶ _____

11 He even designed a helicopter and an airplane.

···▶ _____

12 He was a really busy man!

···▶ _____

Rachel's Busy Day

A Write the meaning of the word in your mother language. Then write the words.

1 assist

_____

2 complain

_____

3 satisfied

_____

4 shrimp

_____

5 supply

_____

6 throw away

_____

B Choose the meaning for each underlined word.

1 Rachel checks on the food <u>supply</u>.

   (a) taste   (b) amount   (c) price

2 One customer isn't <u>satisfied</u> with his meal.

   (a) pleased   (b) surprised   (c) busy

C Fill in the blanks.

> shrimp   throw away   assist

1 Rachel's three junior chefs _____ her.

2 She needs more _____ and pasta, so she orders them.

3 One chef has to _____ the burnt chicken.

D Unscramble the sentences.

1 at / opens / the restaurant / five / .

...▶ _____

2 special / decides on / she / the day's / .

...▶ _____

3 the soups / starts / preparing / Rachel / .

...▶ _____

4 start / meals / ordering / customers / .

...▶ _____

5 wine / him / gives / a bottle of / she / .

...▶ _____

E Fill in the blanks with 'at,' 'on,' or 'in.'   Grammar

1 Brad always wakes up _____ seven thirty.

2 What do you usually do _____ Christmas Eve?

3 My sister was born _____ 1998.

4 The family is going on a picnic _____ Saturday.

5 We're going to eat dinner _____ six o'clock.

6 They plan to take a trip _____ July.

F Translate each sentence into your mother language.

1 Rachel is a busy woman. She's the head chef at Primo's, a popular Italian restaurant.

⋯▶ _____

2 It opens at five, but she arrives there at noon.

⋯▶ _____

3 First, she decides on the day's special: shrimp and pasta in a cream sauce.

⋯▶ _____

4 Then she checks on the food supply. She needs more shrimp and pasta, so she orders them.

⋯▶ _____

5 Around four o'clock, Rachel starts preparing the soups, and her three junior chefs assist her.

⋯▶ _____

6 At five, customers start ordering meals. Suddenly, everyone is really busy.

⋯▶ _____

7 One chef burns the chicken. He has to throw away the chicken.

⋯▶ _____

8 One customer complains. He isn't satisfied with his meal.

⋯▶ _____

9 So Rachel gives him a bottle of wine to make him pleased.

⋯▶ _____

10 At ten o'clock, the restaurant is closed.

⋯▶ _____

11 The junior chefs clean up the kitchen while Rachel plans tomorrow's menu.

⋯▶ _____

12 She's tired but happy that things have gone well.

⋯▶ _____

Jobs of the Future

A Write the meaning of the word in your mother language. Then write the words.

❶ advanced

❷ industry

❸ society

❹ space

❺ technology

❻ tourism

B Choose the meaning for each underlined word.

❶ There will be lots of new jobs in the <u>tourism</u> industry.

ⓐ travel business   ⓑ banking business   ⓒ hotel business

❷ Our society gets more <u>advanced</u>.

ⓐ boring   ⓑ developed   ⓒ interesting

C Fill in the blanks.

> technology   space   industry

❶ Humans may start traveling in _____.

❷ There will be many jobs using _____.

❸ People get older, so there will be many jobs in health care _____.

D Unscramble the sentences.

1 be / there / new jobs / will / .

···▸ _____

2 used to / ice / some people / deliver / .

···▸ _____

3 have / more free / people / time / .

···▸ _____

4 have to / for / people / will / study / a long time / .

···▸ _____

5 can / a spaceship / you / become / cleaner / !

···▸ _____

E Rewrite the sentences. Use 'there will be.' Grammar

1 There is rain.

···▸ _____

2 There are ten people at the party.

···▸ _____

3 There is a comedy on TV at seven.

···▸ _____

4 There are some businessmen at the meeting.

···▸ _____

5 There is a camp next Monday.

···▸ _____

6 There is a math test on Tuesday.

···▸ _____

F Translate each sentence into your mother language.

1 As the world changes, people's jobs also change. Some of them disappear, so no one doe
them.

····▶ _____

2 For instance, some people used to deliver ice. But these days, it's not easy to see the 'icem

····▶ _____

3 Instead, there will be new jobs, perhaps more jobs in the future.

····▶ _____

4 People are getting older, so there will be many jobs in health care.

····▶ _____

5 People have more free time and they would take vacations more often.

····▶ _____

6 This means there will be lots of new jobs in the tourism industry.

····▶ _____

7 Every year, our society gets more advanced. So there will be many jobs using technology.

····▶ _____

8 People will have to study for a long time before they can do them.

····▶ _____

9 And soon, humans may start traveling in space.

····▶ _____

10 There will be jobs on the moon in the future.

····▶ _____

11 Maybe you can become a spaceship cleaner on the moon!

····▶ _____

The Miser and His Gold

A Write the meaning of the word in your mother language. Then write the words.

1 alone

_____

2 bury

_____

3 coin

_____

4 lock

_____

5 miser

_____

6 overhear

_____

B Choose the meaning for each underlined word.

1 The <u>miser</u> went to see his money.

ⓐ greedy person ⓑ poor person ⓒ kind person

2 An old miser once lived <u>alone</u>.

ⓐ loudly ⓑ together ⓒ with no one

C Fill in the blanks.

overheard   buried   coins

1 The miser had hundreds of gold _____.

2 He _____ the box in his backyard.

3 He spoke too loudly, so a thief walking outside _____ him.

D Unscramble the sentences.

1 a wife / have / he / didn't / .

···▸ _____

2 never / he / his money / spent / .

···▸ _____

3 the fence / he / the gold / climed / and took / .

···▸ _____

4 his gold / he / in a box / locked / .

···▸ _____

5 anything / neighbors / see / couldn't / his / .

···▸ _____

E Match the sentences with ones that use possessive pronouns. Grammar

1 That's your backpack. •   • ⓐ That is theirs.

2 This is my watch. •   • ⓑ These are hers.

3 That is Tom and Ed's bike. •   • ⓒ These are mine.

4 These are her toys. •   • ⓓ That's yours.

5 Those are our books. •   • ⓔ Those are ours.

6 These are my papers. •   • ⓕ This is mine.

F Translate each sentence into your mother language.

1 An old miser once lived alone. He didn't have a wife, children, or any friends.

...▶ _____

2 However, he had hundreds of gold coins. But he never spent his money.

...▶ _____

3 Instead, he locked his gold in a box and buried it in his backyard.

...▶ _____

4 Every Friday, the miser went to his backyard and dug up the box of coins.

...▶ _____

5 He said, "It's my gold! It's all mine, mine, mine!"

...▶ _____

6 He did this at night, so his neighbors couldn't see anything.

...▶ _____

7 However, one night, the miser was speaking too loudly, so a thief walking outside overheard him.

...▶ _____

8 The thief waited until the miser went to bed.

...▶ _____

9 Then he climbed the fence, dug up the box, and took the gold.

...▶ _____

10 The next Friday, the miser went to see his box. He saw a huge hole in the ground.

...▶ _____

11 "Oh, no!" he cried, "Someone has stolen my money!"

...▶ _____

Unit 10 Who Donated the Money?

A Write the meaning of the word in your mother language. Then write the words.

1 anonymous

2 donation

3 financial

4 homeless

5 lose

6 receive

B Choose the meaning for each underlined word.

1 Many donors prefer to remain <u>anonymous</u>.

ⓐ unnamed   ⓑ helpful   ⓒ famous

2 There were many people at a <u>homeless</u> center.

ⓐ financial   ⓑ having a house   ⓒ not having a house

C Fill in the blanks.

donations   lost   financial

1 Sometimes people don't have enough money. Maybe they _____ their jobs.

2 They often receive _____ from others.

3 One family had some _____ problems. They couldn't buy anything.

D Unscramble the sentences.

1 knows / nobody / names / their / .

…▸ _____

2 gave / he / each person / to / $100 / .

…▸ _____

3 gave / them / the presents / who / ?

…▸ _____

4 Santa Claus / like / he / was dressed / .

…▸ _____

5 over / the center / 350 people / there were / at / .

…▸ _____

E Fill in the blanks with the question words. **Grammar**

| what | when | who | how | where | why |

1 _____ baked the cake? - I baked the cake.

2 _____ are we going? - We're going to the park.

3 _____ was the movie? - The movie was great.

4 _____ are they doing now? - They're eating dinner now.

5 _____ is John visiting? - John is visiting this Friday.

6 _____ do you like computer games? - Because they're fun.

F Translate each sentence into your mother language.

1 Sometimes people don't have enough money.

···▶ _____

2 Maybe they lost their jobs or had to spend lots of money at the hospital.

···▶ _____

3 In these cases, they often receive donations from others.

···▶ _____

4 Many donors prefer to remain anonymous. This means nobody knows their names.

···▶ _____

5 Last year, around Christmas, one family had some financial problems.

···▶ _____

6 They couldn't buy any presents for their children. But, on Christmas Day, they got a phone call.

···▶ _____

7 The person just said, "Look outside." In front of their house were two big bags of presents.

···▶ _____

8 Who gave them the presents? No one knows.

···▶ _____

9 A few years ago, there were many people at a homeless center.

···▶ _____

10 Suddenly, a man drove up in his car. He was dressed like Santa Claus.

···▶ _____

11 He gave $100 to each person there. There were over 350 people at the center.

···▶ _____

12 What was the man's name? No one knows.

···▶ _____

The World's Richest Man

A Write the meaning of the word in your mother language. Then write the words.

❶ electronics _____ _____

❷ employee _____ _____

❸ own _____ _____

❹ salary _____ _____

❺ share _____ _____

❻ wealthy _____ _____

B Choose the meaning for each underlined word.

❶ There was once a <u>wealthy</u> man named John Dollar.

ⓐ healthy ⓑ rich ⓒ tired

❷ He <u>owned</u> an electronics company.

ⓐ had ⓑ started ⓒ gave

C Fill in the blanks.

| salaries | sharing | employees |

❶ John made his _____ work very hard.

❷ He raised their _____.

❸ He started _____ his money with everyone.

D Unscramble the sentences.

1 have / I / money / enough / .

···▶ _____

2 we / any breaks / get / never / .

···▶ _____

3 everyone / to / I / be happy / want / .

···▶ _____

4 in the world / he / the richest / was / man / .

···▶ _____

5 wrong / what's / everyone / with / ?

···▶ _____

E Unscramble the sentences. Grammar

1 made / he / me / smile / . _____

2 laugh / she / us / makes / . _____

3 I / a pizza / made / him / order / . _____

4 made / they / the window / us / close / . _____

5 me / made / Kevin / again / try / . _____

6 learn / makes / he / his children / the piano / . _____

F Translate each sentence into your mother language.

1 There was once a wealthy man named John Dollar. He owned an electronics company.

····▶ _____

2 He loved money, so he worked and worked every day. He also made his employees work very hard.

····▶ _____

3 John became richer and richer. Soon, he was the richest man in the world.

····▶ _____

4 One day, John was walking through his company. "You there," he said to a worker.

····▶ _____

5 "Why aren't the employees smiling? What's wrong with everyone?" he asked.

····▶ _____

6 The worker answered, "We're tired because we never get any breaks. We work hard, but we're still very poor."

····▶ _____

7 John went home and thought about what the worker said. The next day, he called a meeting.

····▶ _____

8 "I have enough money," he said. "Now I want everyone to be happy."

····▶ _____

9 John gave his employees the day off. Then he raised their salaries.

····▶ _____

10 He started sharing his money with everyone.

····▶ _____

11 And the workers at his company became happier and happier.

····▶ _____

The History of Money.

A Write the meaning of the word in your mother language. Then write the words.

1 carry

2 check

3 firewood

4 melt

5 metal

6 trade

B Choose the meaning for each underlined word.

1 People <u>traded</u> with each other.

ⓐ exchanged　　ⓑ fought　　ⓒ bought

2 Some people don't even <u>carry</u> money now!

ⓐ spend　　ⓑ make　　ⓒ bring

C Fill in the blanks.

| metals　　melt　　checks |

1 People learned how to _____ metal.

2 These days, people use _____ and credit cards.

3 They made coins from gold, silver, copper, and other _____.

D Unscramble the sentences.

1 money / was / no / there / .

...▸ _____

2 for money / used / people / animals / .

...▸ _____

3 buy / with / they / no money / things / .

...▸ _____

4 shells / used / people / as money / .

...▸ _____

5 paper money / began to / some countries / use / .

...▸ _____

E Rewrite the sentences. Use 'how to.' Grammar

1 My brother knows (do taekwondo)

...▸ _____

2 Janet learned (drive a car)

...▸ _____

3 I am studying (play the piano)

...▸ _____

4 They are learning (speak Chinese)

...▸ _____

5 Do you know (surf the Internet)

...▸ _____

6 Kevin knows (play baseball)

...▸ _____

F Translate each sentence into your mother language.

1 A long time ago, there was no money. Then people bartered goods.

····▶ _____

2 That means they traded with each other.

····▶ _____

3 Maybe a person traded four apples for three oranges. Or another person traded shoes for firewood.

····▶ _____

4 Later, people used animals for money. They bought items with cows, pigs, horses, and chickens.

····▶ _____

5 And in some cultures, people used shells as money. In fact, some places in Africa still use them today.

····▶ _____

6 People then learned how to melt metal. So they could make coins.

····▶ _____

7 They made coins from gold, silver, copper, and other metals.

····▶ _____

8 Gold and silver coins were popular for hundreds of years.

····▶ _____

9 Later, some countries began to use paper money.

····▶ _____

10 These days, we use both coins and paper money.

····▶ _____

11 But people also use checks and credit cards. They can buy things with no money.

····▶ _____

12 So some people don't even carry money now!

····▶ _____

The Little Prince

A Write the meaning of the word in your mother language. Then write the words.

1 bite

2 desert

3 encounter

4 lie

5 odd

6 planet

B Choose the meaning for each underlined word.

1 The prince thought all of them were <u>odd</u>.

ⓐ good   ⓑ lonely   ⓒ strange

2 He <u>encountered</u> a businessman and a lamplighter.

ⓐ met   ⓑ knew   ⓒ sent

C Fill in the blanks.

planets   bit   lied

1 The prince decided to visit other _____.

2 The prince loved his rose, but she _____ to him once.

3 The snake _____ the prince, who died.

D Unscramble the sentences.

1 a planet / on / a little prince / lived / .

...▶ _____

2 started / rose / growing / a/ .

...▶ _____

3 the prince / in / the desert / landed / .

...▶ _____

4 his / to see / he / rose / wanted / .

...▶ _____

5 it / him back / to his planet / could / send / .

...▶ _____

E Combine the two sentences. Use 'and.' *Grammar*

1 He likes to watch television. He likes to play sports.

...▶ _____

2 My mother wants to cook dinner. My mother wants to clean the house.

...▶ _____

3 I plan to meet my friends. I plan to have fun.

...▶ _____

4 Emily wants to buy a bag. Emily wants to sell a pen.

...▶ _____

5 They decided to go home. They decided to get some rest.

...▶ _____

6 We want to go on a picnic. We want to play baseball.

...▶ _____

F Translate each sentence into your mother language.

① A little prince once lived on a planet. One day, a rose started growing there.

···▶ _____

② The prince loved his rose, but she lied to him once.

···▶ _____

③ So he decided to leave and visit other planets.

···▶ _____

④ While visiting other planets, the prince met some strange people on them.

···▶ _____

⑤ On the first planet, he met a king. On another planet, he met a drunk.

···▶ _____

⑥ He also encountered a businessman and a lamplighter.

···▶ _____

⑦ The prince thought all of them were odd.

···▶ _____

⑧ Then the prince arrived on Earth and landed in the desert.

···▶ _____

⑨ After some time, he became lonely and wanted to see his rose again.

···▶ _____

⑩ A snake told the prince it could send him back to his planet.

···▶ _____

⑪ And the snake bit the prince, who died.

···▶ _____

⑫ Then the prince and his rose were together again.

···▶ _____

Aliens in Stories and Movies

A Write the meaning of the word in your mother language. Then write the words.

1 alien

_____

2 destroy

_____

3 fiction

_____

4 mean

_____

5 monstrous

_____

6 murder

_____

B Choose the meaning for each underlined word.

1 In movies, aliens are often <u>mean</u>.

ⓐ wealthy   ⓑ unfriendly   ⓒ kind

2 The aliens tried to <u>destroy</u> Earth.

ⓐ imagine   ⓑ ruin   ⓒ help

C Fill in the blanks.

fiction   murder   aliens

1 There are also good _____, like in *E.T.*

2 In _____, there are many different kinds of aliens.

3 In lots of stories, aliens attack and _____ humans.

D Unscramble the sentences.

1 alone / we / are / ?

...▸ _____

2 often / aliens / imagine / writers / .

...▸ _____

3 humans / they / to attack / Earth / visit / .

...▸ _____

4 English / to speak / the alien / learned / .

...▸ _____

5 to / they / seemed / humans / friendly / .

...▸ _____

E Answer the questions with sentences using 'no one.' Grammar

1 How many people are in the room?

...▸ _____

2 Who talked to the teacher?

...▸ _____

3 Who stole the money?

...▸ _____

4 How many people watched the movie?

...▸ _____

5 Who ate the piece of pizza?

...▸ _____

6 How many people will go on the picnic?

...▸ _____

F Translate each sentence into your mother language.

1 Are we alone? Many people have looked at the stars and wondered that.

···▶ _____

2 No one knows if there are aliens or not. But writers and filmmakers often imagine aliens.

···▶ _____

3 In fact, in fiction, there are many different kinds of aliens.

···▶ _____

4 In lots of stories, the aliens are unfriendly. They often visit Earth to attack and murder humans.

···▶ _____

5 This happened in H.G. Well's *The War of the Worlds*.

···▶ _____

6 Martians came to Earth and killed many people. In the end though, all of the aliens died.

···▶ _____

7 Also, in movies, aliens are often mean. The creature in *Alien* was a monstrous alien.

···▶ _____

8 The aliens in *Independence Day* tried to destroy Earth.

···▶ _____

9 But there are also good aliens. Sometimes, like in *E.T.*, they just visited Earth.

···▶ _____

10 They seemed curious and friendly to humans.

···▶ _____

11 Even more, the alien in *E.T.* learned to speak English by repeating what humans say.

···▶ _____

A Visit to Mars

A Write the meaning of the word in your mother language. Then write the words.

1 astronaut _____ _____

2 communicate _____ _____

3 land _____ _____

4 Mars _____ _____

5 peace _____ _____

6 translate _____ _____

B Choose the meaning for each underlined word.

1 The computer can <u>communicate</u> with Martians.

    ⓐ fight   ⓑ travel   ⓒ speak

2 We come in <u>peace</u>.

    ⓐ no running   ⓑ no fighting or war   ⓒ no speaking

C Fill in the blanks.

land	translate	astronauts

1 We're about to _____ on Mars!

2 The three _____ on *Eagle 1* were excited.

3 I hope the computer can _____ for us.

D Unscramble the sentences.

1 are / we / Earth / from / .

...▸ _____

2 they / what / saying / are / ?

...▸ _____

3 opened / of / they / the doors / the spaceship / .

...▸ _____

4 seem / good people / you / like / .

...▸ _____

5 the first people / were / the planet / to visit / they / .

...▸ _____

E Circle the adjectives in the correct order. Grammar

1 An elephant is a (huge gray, gray huge) animal.

2 My sister has a (yellow big, big yellow) bag.

3 He is holding a (round small, small round) phone.

4 She has a (tiny brown, brown tiny) dog.

5 She has (black long, long black) hair.

6 I just bought a (red rectangular, rectangular red) carpet.

F Translate each sentence into your mother language.

1 "We're about to land on Mars!" said Tina, the head astronaut.

...▸ _____

2 The three astronauts on *Eagle 1* were excited since they were the first people to visit the planet.

...▸ _____

3 "Look, there are Martians down there," said Lewis.

...▸ _____

4 There were several tiny green people below. They had three arms, four legs, and two heads each!

...▸ _____

5 "I hope the computer can communicate with them and translate for us," said George.

...▸ _____

6 They landed on Mars and opened the doors of the spaceship.

...▸ _____

7 The Martians looked at them and started making funny noises.

...▸ _____

8 "What are they saying?" said Tina.

...▸ _____

9 The computer answered, "They think you look silly because you only have one head."

...▸ _____

10 "We are from Earth. We come in peace," said Tina. The Martian leader smiled at them.

...▸ _____

11 "Even though you have one head, you seem like good people," he answered.

...▸ _____

12 Then Earthlings and Martians became great friends.

...▸ _____

Apollo 11

A Write the meaning of the word in your mother language. Then write the words.

1 act

2 amazing

3 hero

4 launch

5 reach

6 satellite

B Choose the meaning for each underlined word.

1 On July 16, 1969, the United States <u>launched</u> Apollo 11.

ⓐ sent off   ⓑ cut off   ⓒ fell off

2 It was an <u>amazing</u> act.

ⓐ common   ⓑ various   ⓒ incredible

C Fill in the blanks.

reach   heroes   satellite

1 The Soviet Union sent a _____ into space.

2 It took them four days to _____ the moon.

3 Neil Armstrong and the other two astronauts were all _____.

D Unscramble the sentences.

1 on / landed / Apollo 11 / the moon.

⋯▶ _____

2 returned / the astronauts / Earth / to / .

⋯▶ _____

3 in / three men / the spaceship / there were / .

⋯▶ _____

4 tried / they / to the moon / men / sending / .

⋯▶ _____

5 people / watched / the moon landing / millions of / .

⋯▶ _____

E Circle the correct prepositions.

Grammar

1 The bus is going (around, through) the corner now.

2 He is going (through, into) his office on the third floor.

3 Tell me when you come (out of, around) the classroom.

4 Walk (through, out of) the intersection and go straight two blocks.

5 A bat suddenly flew (out of, around) the cave.

6 You have to run (into, around) the tree twice.

F Translate each sentence into your mother language.

1 In 1957, the Soviet Union sent a satellite into space.

....▶ _____

2 Then, the USA and Soviet Union began the space race.

....▶ _____

3 First, they sent satellites into space. Then, they sent animals and people there.

....▶ _____

4 Finally, they tried sending men to the moon.

....▶ _____

5 In the 1960s, the United States worked hard on the space program. It spent very much money on it.

....▶ _____

6 On July 16, 1969, it launched *Apollo 11*. There were three men in the spaceship.

....▶ _____

7 It took them four days to reach the moon. Then, on July 20, *Apollo 11* landed on the moon.

....▶ _____

8 Neil Armstrong became the first man to set foot on it.

....▶ _____

9 Another astronaut, Buzz Aldrin, walked on the moon with him.

....▶ _____

10 On Earth, millions of people watched the moon landing. It was an amazing act.

....▶ _____

11 A few days later, on July 24, the astronauts returned to Earth. They were all heroes!

....▶ _____